Is John Piper an Antinomian?

This study contends that John Piper, the hugely popular promoter of Christian Hedonism, is an antinomian. This claim is based on his own words. The starting point of the case against Piper must be the 'Ask Pastor John' (APJ) interview recorded in 2010, when he was asked the straight-forward question, 'Are Christians under the Ten Commandments?'

His response was unequivocal: 'No! The Bible says we're not under the law.' But Piper relied in his answer on what many see as the proof text for antinomianism, namely Romans 6.14—he used part of this verse out of context: 'we're not under the law.'

The term 'antinomianism' was used for the first time by Martin Luther. It is the belief that Christians are no longer under the Ten Commandments (or the moral law) as a rule of life. Historic Christianity has always regarded antinomianism as a heresy. Yet antinomianism is vital to John Piper's radical new doctrine of Christian Hedonism, first presented in his 1986 book, *Desiring God*. This charge is not made lightly. Clear and compelling evidence, taken from Piper's own words, is presented to substantiate this claim.

Dr Williams was Director of Public Health for Croydon Health Authority (UK) for many years. He is the author of: *Christian Hedonism? A biblical examination of John Piper's teaching* (2017); *Holistic Mission: Weighed in the Balances* (2016); *The New Calvinists* (2014); *The Dark Side of Christian Counselling* (2009), and several other books on contempary Christian issues.

ISBN 978-0-9954845-2-8

Belmont House Publishing
36 The Crescent, Belmont
Sutton, Surrey, SM2 6BJ
ISBN: 978-0-9954845-2-8

9 780995 484528

Is John Piper an Antinomian?

E S Williams

Belmont House Publishing

London

Is John Piper an Antinomian?

Published by Belmont House Publishing, London

First published March 2018

ISBN 978-0-9954845-2-8

Scripture quotations from the Authorised King James Version of the Holy Bible.

Desiring God quotes from the 2011 edition

Published by Belmont House Publishing
36 The Crescent
Belmont
SUTTON
Surrey SM2 6BJ

Website www.belmonthouse.co.uk

A Catalogue record for this book is available from the British Library.

Five YouTube videos on John Piper's ministry are available for viewing on the New Calvinist website: www.newcalvinist.com/
John Piper in the Dark
Piper's Journey into Hedonism
The Folly of Christian Hedonism
Is John Piper an Antinomian?
John Piper's Hero—C.S. Lewis

Printed by Marston Book Services Ltd, Didcot, UK

Is John Piper an Antinomian?

Table of Contents

Foreword

Dr John Piper has been one of the most influential theologians over the last thirty years.

His effect has been felt not only among churches within the Reformed constituency but has touched people in the charismatic movement and beyond. Piper has used the annual Passion Conference in Atlanta, Georgia, attended by tens of thousands of young people, to propagate his philosophy of Christian Hedonism, and also to endorse Passion's worldly style of contemporary worship, which includes the worst excesses of Christian 'rap' and 'holy hip-hop'.

For many years the Pastor of Bethlehem Baptist Church in Minneapolis, his teaching has reached this very wide audience as a result of his prolific writing and the popularity of his website, Desiring God. Best known for his book of that name, *Desiring God: Meditations of a Christian Hedonist* (1986), Dr Piper has also been a frequent speaker at conferences throughout the western world and further afield.

In 2010, a book was published to which a host of esteemed writers contributed – *For the Fame of God's Name: Essays in Honor of John Piper.* Not many churchmen have received such a tribute while still alive. But John Piper has.

My own travels with John Piper began in the mid-1990s. As a recent émigré from a charismatic church, I had sought and found spiritual sanctuary among the ranks of the Reformed churches. Having witnessed at first hand the so-called 'Toronto Blessing', a charismatic experience causing people to perform bizarre antics and linked to a host of highly questionable teachings and teachers, I might have thought the churches imbued with the spirit of Luther, Calvin, Whitefield and Spurgeon would have been immune to the attractions of such outrageous teachings, claims and behaviour.

Not so.

Instead I found many people impressed with the ministry of Dr Piper, even though he was on record stating his appreciation of what the Toronto Blessing had brought to him. Extraordinary! And many, who I thought would have been as shocked as me, supported his ministry, including the teaching he is most associated with—Christian Hedonism.

This brings us to the book that is now in your hand.

Dr Ted Williams has carefully documented one of the core errors at the heart of Dr Piper's ministry – antinomianism. He has already taken a close look at Christian Hedonism and found it wanting (see his *Christian Hedonism? A biblical examination of John Piper's teaching*). Here he narrows his focus to consider an age-old error that has always afflicted the true church – the belief that the Christian is discharged from obeying the moral law or Ten Commandments. Dr Williams proves his thesis that Dr Piper is an antinomian with unerring accuracy and with close reference to Dr Piper's actual teaching.

In doing this our author has performed an admirable service for the Church. If you are setting out to exonerate Dr Piper of the charge, I do not envy you. The evidence Dr Williams presents here is overwhelming. We all need to read it carefully.

Pastor Chris Hand, Crich Baptist Church,
Derbyshire, UK.
Author of *Falling Short? The Alpha Course Examined* (Day One Publications, 1998)

Chapter 1

Ask Pastor John

John Piper is no stranger to controversy. In his best-selling book, *Desiring God*, first published in 1986, he introduced his new radical doctrine of Christian Hedonism to the Christian world. He has since spent three decades promoting this novel doctrine throughout the USA and across the world. Indeed his popularity as a celebrity preacher knows no bounds; today he is perhaps the most famous preacher in America and well received beyond. His influence has become truly global.

This study asks a simple question: Is John Piper an antinomian? This is an extremely serious question, for antinomianism has been considered by most Bible-believing Christians down the centuries to be a heresy. It follows that an accusation of antinomianism cannot be lightly made. My purpose in this study is to provide the evidence on which the charge of antinomianism is levelled against John Piper and his ministry, using his own words.

Antinomianism

So what is antinomianism and why is it so important? The word antinomian is from the Greek and means 'against the law' (*anti* – against; *nomos* – law). It may be briefly defined as the doctrine that holds that God's moral law (the Ten Commandments) is not binding on Christians as a rule of life. An antinomian believes that because a Christian is under grace, he is no longer under God's moral law as expressed in the Ten Commandments. This doctrinal error effectively opens the door to all kinds of problems, and exposes the believer to a wrong understanding of sanctification and even to moral failure. It removes the objective biblical expression of God's holy character as set out in the moral imperatives of the Ten Commandments; and it leaves the believer a prey to subjective and unbiblical methods of sanctification. In its worst manifestation it is a justification for ungodly living.

We're not Under the Law

The starting point of the case against Piper must be the 'Ask Pastor John' (APJ) interview recorded in 2010, when he was asked the straightforward question, 'Are Christians under the Ten Commandments?'

His response is unequivocal: 'No! The Bible says we're not under the law.' Piper has relied on what many see as the 'proof text' for antinomianism, namely Romans 6.14—and in his answer he uses part of this verse out of context: 'We're not under the law'.[1]

In *The Law and the Gospel* (1997), Ernest Reisinger, a Reformed Baptist pastor and author, comments: 'one of the most misquoted, misunderstood, and misapplied verses in all the Bible is Romans 6.14. The second part of the verse is usually quoted out of context: "You are not under the law but under grace". Quoting only that part of the verse while ignoring the first clause ("Sin shall not have dominion over you") distorts the meaning of the passage altogether. To do so is to separate what God has joined together, and the sad result of this separation is a generation of lost, lawless, antinomian church members.'[2]

So Romans 6.14 must be interpreted in its wider context. In chapters 3 and 4 of Romans, Paul has demonstrated that a sinner is justified by faith in Christ alone, not by the works of the law. He triumphantly concludes: 'Therefore being justified by faith, we have peace with God through our Lord Jesus Christ: by whom also we have access by faith into this grace wherein we stand, and rejoice in hope of the glory of God' (Romans 5.1-2). In chapter 6 Paul deals with the objection that the doctrine of justification by faith alone encourages sin. 'Shall we continue in sin, that grace may abound? God forbid. How shall we, that are dead to sin, live any longer therein?' (Romans 6.1-2). Paul explains that our old man, that is, our sinful nature, is crucified with Christ, 'that the body of sin might be destroyed, that henceforth we should not serve sin. For he that is dead is freed from sin' (verses 6-7). And so, in view of this great truth, we come to verse 14 referred to by Piper above—a believer who stands in God's grace should not let sin dominate his life: 'but yield yourselves unto God, as those that are alive from the dead, and your members as instruments of righteousness unto God. For sin shall not have dominion over you: for ye are not under the law, but under grace' (Romans 6.13-14). In the context of Paul's argument, verse 14 is stating a great spiritual truth—sin shall not have *dominion* in the life of a true believer. As a justified sinner, you should not let sin *reign* in your mortal body and you should not present your members as instruments of unrighteousness, for sin shall not have dominion over you. And the reason sin shall not have dominion is because you are under the grace of God, not under the law of sin and death. In Romans 6.14 Reisinger explains that 'Paul describes those who are no longer dominated by sin because they are no longer under the law of sin'.[3] Formerly the law could only reveal and condemn our sin, but now we have the new power, through the indwelling Holy Spirit, acting upon our regenerated nature, to prevent its reign in us—this is the grace Paul speaks of in verse 14. Now the moral law is become our cherished and indispensable guide to a sanctified life, for we are no longer slaves to sin. That this is Paul's meaning is confirmed by passages like Romans 13.8-10 and 1 Corinthians 7.19. Piper's use of Romans 6.14 is antinomian and totally wrong.

Arthur Pink, author of *The Sovereignty of God*, comments: 'The force of Romans 6.14 becomes more apparent if we observe what follows it. In the very next verse we read, "What then? Shall we sin, because we are not under the law, but under grace? God forbid". This anticipates an objection: If we are not under the Law as the ground of our justification, then are we to be lawless? The inspired answer is, God forbid. Nothing is more self-evidently certain then, that if the moral Law is not a rule of life to believers, they are at liberty to disregard its precepts. But the apostle rejects this error with the utmost abhorrence.'[4]

It's Under Us

Turning again to the APJ video, we hear Piper deal with the question: 'Now, shall we sin that grace may abound? Paul says dead men don't sin. If you died to sin, how can you still live in it, meaning that new birth is the writing of the law on the heart, so that we are not under it, *it's under us*, it's just coming out. So the way we strive toward being obedient, holy, loving people, is not by getting up in the morning and pulling the list out of our pocket—okay, and there's the list and I'm off to do them[...] We stake our lives in the Gospel and then instead of serving the law we serve one another in love. Love is the fruit of faith in Jesus, faith working through love, and if you ask what love looks like, 1 John says it keeps the commandments. Which commandments? Well, the ones that are loving. "Love God and do as you please" is not bad advice if you are bent on holiness, if you are bent on love.' Piper continues: 'The Ten Commandments are really important, you should hang them on your wall and you should measure your life by them, *but in a very different way* than when you were under them, because they have been kept for you. You are now married to the risen Christ, not married to the law. And not in the oldness of the letter but the newness of the Spirit. Our whole approach toward transformation and love and life is different than list-keeping' (emphasis added).

Firstly, we note Piper again says we are not under the law that is now written on the heart, it is under us. So in his opinion born-again believers effectively stand above the law given at Mount Sinai. We note his dismissive attitude towards the Ten Commandments, which he mockingly refers to as a list which we keep in our pocket. He then draws a false dichotomy between serving the law and serving one another. But it is the moral law – don't steal, don't lie, don't covet, for instance – which teaches us how to serve others. So keeping the law and serving others are not in opposition. We do not choose the one above the other—an obedient believer serves both; for the law of love (the moral law) shows us the real meaning of love.

Secondly, we note Piper says we should keep the Commandments which are *loving*, but he does not identify the Commandments he thinks are unloving, which, by inference, we don't need to keep. Of course, all the Ten Commandments are loving—the product of God's loving character.

Thirdly, while Piper refers to the Ten Commandments as 'really important', and says we should hang them on the wall and 'measure' our lives by them, he quickly qualifies this with a very significant statement—'but in a very different way than when you were under them'. He has again reminded us that we are not under the Ten Commandments and therefore the way we measure our lives by them is now very different. This is a far cry from an explicit and unequivocal commitment to obey God's moral law as a rule of life. There is a reason for his reluctance to call for obedience to the Ten Commandments—his antinomian stance is essential to his doctrine of Christian Hedonism, the central teaching of his ministry. In his scheme for Christian living, sanctification is the by-product of 'desiring' God above all created things. To grow in sanctification we must 'desire' God above all things in a hedonistic manner—seeking maximum pleasure in Him 24/7, as Piper puts it. So law-keeping is secondary at best, and positively harmful if it replaces the much more essential 'desiring God' and finding all our pleasure and happiness in Him. As Piper has said: 'Love God and do as you please' is not bad advice.

Christian Hedonism is dealt with more fully in my book, *Christian Hedonism? A biblical examination of John Piper's teaching* (2017).

Are Christians Called to Obey the Law?

In another APJ interview in 2013, Piper responds to the question: 'Are Christians called to obey the law?' He correctly explains that justification is by faith and not by law-keeping. He then addresses the question: 'What do we do with the Commandments? What is the use of the Commandments for the Christian?'[5]

Piper says: 'The Commandments never can make God to be for us—He is already for us, in Christ. We're in Christ, so no commandment-keeping can make us acceptable to God. We are acceptable in Christ, *which puts commandment-keeping at a lower level*—the way to live the Christian life is not by focusing on Commandments. They can help discern the path of love, but the key to living the Christian life is very different than a *focus on commandment-keeping* towards pleasing God and bringing us 100% into His favor' (emphasis added).

Here Piper has downgraded commandment-keeping to a lower level. He is adamant that Christians should not make it the focus of their life to be obedient to God's Ten Commandments. Indeed, Piper even infers that obeying God's Commandments is not 'the way to live the Christian life'.

He continues: 'And the key verse which I love so much that I try to live in it each day is Romans 7.6: "Now we are released from the law, having died to that which held us captive". So we died to the law and are *no longer under the law*. We are no longer its slaves, so that we may serve – oh yes, there is a serving – in the new way of the Spirit not the old way of the letter; the letter kills, the Spirit gives life' (emphasis added). He interprets Romans 7.6 to mean that Christians are released from the law and therefore no longer under it. But this is a partial truth, for we have not become *lawless*. While believers are completely freed from the law as a covenant of works, as a way of salvation, they are still under the moral law as a rule of life.

Matthew Henry's Concise Commentary explains Romans 7.6: 'Believers are delivered from that power of the law, which condemns for the sins committed by them. And they are delivered from that power of the law which stirs up and provokes the sin that dwells in them. *Understand this not of the law as a rule, but as a covenant of works.* In profession and privilege, we are under a covenant of grace, and not under a covenant of works; under the gospel of Christ, not under the law of Moses' (emphasis added).

Yes we are under grace, thank God, but that does not mean that we are *lawless* and should stop obeying the law of God found in the Ten Commandments. We are no longer under the law of sin and death, as Christ Jesus has freed us from this law, the law of the flesh.

Piper's Take on Antinomianism

In June 2014 in another APJ, Piper responded to the question: 'Pastor John, can our emphasis on gospel-centered sanctification, rooted in our justification, lead to antinomianism?'[6] Piper said: 'So on this issue of justification and sanctification the term 'antinomianism' is often not defined enough for me to know what to say. I am not sure what people are referring to when they talk about it. It contains the word law, "no-mian"; and "anti" means against, or in the place of. So it can mean a person is against the law as a way of salvation. But what is in mind with the word "law" here? All imperatives? Mosaic Law? Whole Old Testament? Ceremonial law? Ethnic Jewish markers? And what is meant by the word "way" in "way of salvation"? Do they mean law-keeping as a way of earning salvation? Or do they mean "way" in the sense of path, so that they are saying: We don't even walk in the path of love which is a fulfillment of all the law?

'So I just want to scream sometimes and say: Oh, for definitions, please, definitions! Does "antinomian" mean anti-godliness, anti-holiness of life, anti-fruit of the Holy Spirit, anti-obedience of faith? It would be a lot clearer if people said what they precisely mean, if they are going to accuse somebody of being antinomian or if they are going to distance themselves from antinomianism. I am just constantly crying out for definitions and for freedom from ambiguities in the absence of these kinds of failed or absent definitions.'

Piper's main point seems to be that he is unclear about what an antinomian really is, because he feels it has not been clearly defined. He says: 'I am not sure what people are referring to when they talk about it'. Piper compounds the ignorance of his position by asking, 'But what is in mind with the word "law" here?' He then mentions the Mosaic Law, whole Old Testament, ceremonial law, ethnic Jewish markers. Remarkably, in this discussion of antinomianism he does not even mention the Ten Commandments or God's moral law. Piper, it seems, is unable, or unwilling, to provide any proper understanding of antinomianism. Is this because if he had done so he would have identified himself as an antinomian? Indeed, he had an ideal opportunity to distance himself from antinomianism—but he did not do so.

Conclusion

In seeking to answer our question regarding Piper and antinomianism, we have uncovered two important issues. First, it is clear from the above analysis that Piper is adamant believers are not under the Ten Commandments, for we are under grace. He also teaches that 'We are acceptable in Christ, which puts commandment-keeping at a lower level—the way to live the Christian life is not by focusing on commandments.' And he says the Christian life is 'very different than a focus on commandment-keeping towards pleasing God and bringing us 100% into his favor'.

The second issue is that Piper claims to be unclear about what an antinomian really is, for he feels it has not been clearly enough defined.

So to answer our question – Is John Piper an antinomian? – we need to define the concept and understand where the term comes from. We also need to understand the role of God's moral law in the life of a believer. What does Reformation Christianity say about antinomianism?

Endnotes

1. Ask Pastor John, 'Are Christians Under the Ten Commandments?' (2010) https://www.youtube.com/watch?v=xR6l87FiR_8

2. Ernest C. Reisinger, *The Law and the Gospel*, P&R Publishing, 1997, pp125-127

3. Ibid. p127

4. 'The Law and the Saint', by Arthur W. Pink, Negative side, http://reformed.org/ethics/index.html

5. Ask Pastor John, 'Are Christians Called to Obey the Law?' (2013), http://www.desiringgod.org/interviews/are-christians-called-to-obey-the-law,

6. Ask Pastor John, 'Does Justification-Centered Sanctification Lead to Antinomianism?' (2014), http://www.desiringgod.org/interviews/does-justification-centered-sanctification-lead-to-antinomianism

Chapter 2

Oh, For Definitions, Please!

In the previous chapter, we heard John Piper say that the term 'antinomianism' is not defined enough for him to know what to say about it; and we heard his plea for definitions: 'Oh, for definitions, please, definitions!'. Yet it is difficult to understand why Piper, a Reformed theologian, seems to be so ignorant of the meaning of antinomianism, when the subject has been hotly debated in Reformed circles for centuries. Indeed, in *No Holiness, No Heaven! Antinomianism Today*, a Banner of Truth book published in 1986, Richard Alderson writes: 'All modern works of reference, both Christian and secular, agree in defining antinomianism as the view that the Moral Law (the Ten Commandments) is not binding on Christians as a rule of life.'[1]

Even a simple Google search would have enlightened him. According to Google an antinomian 'is a person who believes that Christians are released by grace from the obligation of observing the moral law'. The website 'got Questions?' offers this definition: 'Theologically, antinomianism is the belief that there are no moral laws God expects Christians to obey.'[2]

Baker's Dictionary of Theology (1960), Baker Book House, says the word 'antinomianism' signifies opposition to law. It refers to the doctrine that the moral law is not binding upon Christians as a rule of life.

In *An Exposition of the Westminster Confession of Faith* (1998 edition, first published 1845), Robert Shaw, a Scottish Presbyterian theologian, describes antinomians as those 'who say that believers are released from the obligation of the moral law'.[3]

Martin Luther and Johann Agricola

According to *Encyclopaedia Britannica*, 'The doctrine of antinomianism grew out of the Protestant controversies on the law and the gospel and was first attributed to Luther's collaborator, Johann Agricola (1494-1566), who taught that Christians are freed by grace from the need to obey the Ten Commandments.'[4]

The term 'antinomianism' was used for the first time by Martin Luther to describe Agricola's position on the role of the Decalogue (the Ten Commandments) in the Church. Agricola believed that a Christian's only motive for living a Christian life was love for Christ, asserting that Christians are freed by grace from the need to obey the Ten Commandments. In 1525 he began to openly assert his antinomianism, condemning the law as an unnecessary carry-over from the Old Testament, and as too similar to the Roman Catholic stress on good works. Agricola brashly declared: 'The Decalogue belongs in the courthouse, not in the pulpit... To the gallows with Moses!' The term 'Antinomian Controversy' refers to the sharp disagreement that arose between Luther and Agricola. Luther responded with five disputations and the treatise *Against the Antinomians* (1539), in which he coined the word 'antinomian' to describe Agricola and his followers.[5] At the time, some actually accused Luther of antinomianism. But this was an unjust accusation, for Luther had a deep commitment to the Ten Commandments. He wrote: 'It is most surprising to me that anyone can claim that I reject the law or the Ten Commandments, since there is available, in more than one edition, my exposition of the Ten Commandments, which furthermore are daily preached and practiced in our churches. Furthermore, the commandments are sung in two versions, as well as painted, printed, carved, and recited by the children morning, noon, and night. I know of no manner in which we do not use them... I myself, as old and as learned as I am, recite the commandments daily word for word like a child.'[6]

While Agricola was certainly not a libertine, antinomians like him were known to place a great emphasis on 'love' and saw the law as hostile to grace, love and faith.

The Antinomian Controversy

Lutheran theologian Gary Jepsen, in his essay, 'The Antinomian Controversy Rides Again', writes: 'Thus, although the word "antinomian" per se does not appear in the NT, the word "anomia" appears frequently and its meaning is very similar to antinomianism. However, even more significant for our purpose is the fact that "anomia" – lawlessness – is never referred to favorably in the NT and is in fact almost always condemned.'[7]

Jepsen goes on: 'From the perspective of Luther, antinomianism arose out of an inadequate reading of the gospels. It was seen as a reading of Scripture that missed the Law-Gospel tension, which was so essential to Luther's thought, because it focused only on a watered down sense of the gospel... And so, the real tragedy of antinomianism is that the gospel is ultimately lost. Without a profound sense for "sin, death and the power of the devil", from what does Christ save us? It is little wonder, therefore, that Luther's reaction to antinomianism, with its rejection of the law, was sharp and unyielding. The gospel, in Luther's eyes, was in danger. "If we cast the Law aside," Luther said, "we shall not long retain Christ".'[8]

To understand the essential role of God's moral law as a rule of life for the Christian we need to turn to the great Confessions of the Protestant faith.

Endnotes

1. Richard Alderson, *No Holiness, No Heaven! Antinomianism Today*, Banner of Truth Trust, 1986, p19

2. https://www.gotquestions.org/antinomianism.html

3. Robert Shaw, *An Exposition of the Westminster Confession of Faith*, 1845, Christian Focus Publications, 1998 edition, p245

4. *Encyclopædia Britannica*, 'Antinomianism', https://www.britannica.com/topic/antinomianism#ref43091

5. *Encyclopædia Britannica*, Johann Agricola, https://www.britannica.com/biography/Johann-Agricola

6. Martin Luther, 'Against the Antinomians', 1539. In Luther's Works. Volume 47: Christians in Society IV. Edited by Franklin Sherman. Philadelphia: Fortress Press. 1971. pp 109–115.

7. Pastor Gary Jepsen blog, 'The Antinomian Controversy Rides Again', http://garyjepsen.com/2016/11/10/178/

8. Ibid

Chapter 3

The Moral Law

A closer look at the moral law in Christian thinking will help us place John Piper's views in a proper context. All the great Confessions of the Reformed faith refer to the Ten Commandments (or the moral law) as binding on Christians as a rule of life. Many modern works of reference, both Christian and secular, agree in defining antinomianism as the belief that the moral law is *not* binding on Christians as a rule of life. So an antinomian is one who does not accept the moral law, spiritually understood, as God's blueprint for sanctified Christian living.

In his book, *Antinomianism* (2013), Mark Jones makes the point that 'in orthodox Christianity, imitating Christ as our pattern of holiness is essential to the Christian life… But the antinomians tended not only to ridicule the idea that we must attempt to conform our lives to the pattern of Christ, but also to suggest that any work we perform is not our work but Christ's. The antinomians also rejected the idea that the law, accompanied by the Spirit, is a true means of sanctification.'[1]

Belgic Confession

The *Belgic Confession*, written in 1561, owed its origin to the need for a clear and comprehensive statement of the Reformed faith during a period of prolonged and intense persecution in the Netherlands. Commenting on Article 25 of the *Confession* ('The Abolishing of the Ceremonial Law'), Martyn McGeown, Pastor of Covenant Protestant Reformed Church in Limerick, Ireland, writes: 'In Reformed theology the law of God has an important place and role to play in the life of the church and of the Christian. The law, although as we have seen in no way contributes to our justification or righteousness before God, remains binding upon all sinners, and remains the rule by which Christians are called to live.'[2] The moral law—as it is set out in the Ten Commandments, which in turn are summarised in Christ's command to love God and our neighbour—is the revelation of the unchanging will of God for all those created in His image.

Threefold Use of the Moral Law

In Protestant thinking (both Lutheran and Reformed) the moral law (or Ten Commandments) is seen as having three uses.

The first use is to be a 'mirror' reflecting the perfect righteousness of God and the sinfulness of man (Romans 7.12). 'Therefore by the deeds of the law there shall no flesh be justified in his sight: for by the law is the knowledge of sin' (Romans 3.20). 'But sin, that it might appear sin, working death in me by that which is good; that sin by the commandment might become exceeding sinful' (Romans 7.13). The law, by showing us our need for forgiveness and our danger of damnation, leads us in repentance and faith to Christ. 'Wherefore the law was our schoolmaster to bring us unto Christ, that we might be justified by faith' (Galatians 3.24).

The second use is to restrain evil. Though the law cannot change the heart, it can to some extent inhibit lawlessness by its threats of judgement, especially when backed by a civil code that administers punishment for proven offences. 'For he [the civil ruler] is the minister of God to thee for good. But if thou do that which is evil, be afraid; for he beareth not the sword in vain: for he is the minister of God, a revenger to execute wrath upon him that doeth evil' (Romans 13.4). Thus it secures civil order, and serves to protect the innocent from the unjust.

The third use of the law is as the rule by which believers are instructed in living unto righteousness out of gratitude for the grace they have received from the Lord. It guides believers into the good works that God has planned for them: 'For we are his workmanship, created in Christ Jesus unto good works, which God hath before ordained that we should walk in them' (Ephesians 2.10). The law tells God's children what pleases their heavenly Father. Christ was speaking of this third use of the law when He said that those who become His disciples must be taught to do all that He had commanded (Matthew 28.20), and that obedience to His commands will prove the reality of one's love for Him: 'If ye love me, keep my commandments' (John 14.15). So the Christian is free from the law as a system of salvation by works, but is under the law of Christ as a rule of life.[3]

The denial of the third use of the law, which is widespread in the evangelical circles of our day, is called antinomianism. The antinomian is the one who asserts that the law has been *fully* abrogated by the coming of Christ into the world, for Romans 6.14 says that we are not under the law but under grace. But as we have already seen, the antinomian is misusing Scripture. While the Christian is not under the law as a covenant of works (that is, as a way of salvation), nor as a ministration of condemnation, he is under it as a rule of life and as an objective standard of righteousness.

Calvin on the Moral Law

John Calvin believed that the moral law provided instruction for believers as to what pleases God. For him the third use of the law, as a rule of life for believers, was its principle use. 'The third and principal use, which pertains more closely to the proper purpose of the law, finds its place among believers in whose heart the Spirit of God already lives and reigns. For even though they have the law written and engraved upon their hearts by the finger of God (Jeremiah 31.33; Hebrews 10.16), they have been so moved and quickened through the directing of the Spirit that they long to obey God...'[4]

In the second edition of his *Institutes* in 1539, Calvin commented on certain ignorant persons who 'rashly cast out the whole law of Moses, and bid farewell to the two Tables of the Law. For they think it obviously alien to Christians to hold to a doctrine that contains the "dispensation of death" (2 Corinthians 3.7). Banish this wicked thought from our minds! Moses has admirably taught that the Law, which among sinners can engender nothing but death, ought among saints to have a better and more excellent use.'[5]

In an exposition of the Ten Commandments, Calvin writes, 'the true knowledge of God constrains us to worship him, and... the true knowledge of self leads to genuine humility and self-abasement. The law is the instrument which the Lord uses to bring about both these results... In setting his law before us as a standard of righteousness, God has based every one of its requirements upon his own good pleasure: from this we conclude that nothing is so acceptable to him as obedience to his will… the law was given by God to teach us true righteousness; and that in it no righteousness is taught but obedience to the divine will… [God's law is] the complete standard of righteousness…'[6]

So Calvin's clear teaching is that God's law is the complete standard of true righteousness, and that obedience to God's law is obedience to the divine will, and that the Ten Commandments remain *forever* as a rule of life for the believer.

William Tyndale

William Tyndale (1494-1536) was a brilliant linguist and seminal figure in the Protestant Reformation in the years leading up to his martyrdom. He is celebrated for his masterly translation of the New Testament into English. 'What Tyndale wanted to avoid was the view, later labelled antinomian, which regarded salvation as having no practical ethical demands or requirements, particularly as regards the keeping of biblical law… The grace of God enables our good works to be genuinely our works. We might even put it like this: our works are indeed part of our salvation, but it is God who makes it possible for us to perform those works.'[7] Meaning not salvation by works, for Tyndale held to justification by faith alone, but that the moral law is our rule of life and guide in holiness and good works (Philippians 2.13).

The Westminster Assembly

The Westminster Assembly, a seventeenth-century gathering of Reformed English and Scottish divines, produced both the Shorter and Longer Catechisms and the Westminster Confession of Faith, published 1647 and 1648. These historic documents have had an enormous impact on the Christian world, particularly the Confession.

Of interest to our study is that Piper uses the well-known answer to the first question of the Shorter Catechism, 'Man's chief end is to glorify God, and to enjoy him forever', to support his doctrine of Christian Hedonism. He famously amends the statement by changing the 'and' to 'by', so, 'Man's chief end is to glorify God, *by* enjoying him forever.'

In response to Question 39, 'What is the duty which God requireth of man?', the Shorter Catechism answers: 'The duty which

God requireth of man is *obedience* to his revealed will.' Question 40: 'What did God at first reveal to man for the rule of his obedience?' Answer: 'The rule which God at first revealed to man for his obedience, was *the moral law*.' Question 41: 'Wherein is the moral law summarily comprehended?' Answer: 'The moral law is summarily comprehended in the Ten Commandments' (emphasis added).

So the Shorter Catechism is absolutely clear that God requires obedience to his will revealed in the moral law, comprehended in the Ten Commandments. We need to remember this as we examine Piper's teaching.

Westminster Confession of Faith

We now turn to the Westminster Confession of Faith (1647). Chapter 19, entitled, 'The Law of God', sets forth the classic Reformed view of the law of God, and helps us further to appreciate the significance of Piper's position. The Confession refers to the Ten Commandments as the moral law of God.

Section 1: 'God gave to Adam a law, as a covenant of works [that is, 'do this and you shall live'], by which he bound him, and all his posterity, to personal, entire, exact, and *perpetual obedience*; promising life upon the fulfilling, and threatening death upon the breach of it; and endued him with power and ability to keep it.'

Section 2: 'This law, after his fall, continued to be a perfect rule of righteousness; and, as such, was delivered by God upon Mount Sinai in ten commandments, and written in two tables; the first four commandments containing our *duty* towards God, and the other six our *duty* to man.'

Section 3: 'Besides this law, *commonly called moral*, God was pleased to give to the people of Israel, as a Church under age, ceremonial laws... prefiguring Christ... All which ceremonial laws are now abrogated under the New Testament.'

Section 5: *'The moral law doth for ever bind all,* as well justified persons as others, to the obedience thereof; and that not only in regard of the matter contained in it, but also in respect of the authority of God, the Creator, who gave it. Neither doth Christ in the gospel any way dissolve, but much strengthens this obligation.'

Section 6: 'Although true believers be not under the law, as a covenant of works, to be thereby justified, or condemned; yet is it of great use to them, as well as to others; in that, *as a rule of life inform-ing them of the will of God,* and their *duty*, it directs and binds them to walk accordingly; discovering also the sinful pollutions of their nature, hearts and lives; so as, examining themselves thereby, they may come to further conviction of, humiliation for, and hatred against sin, together with a clearer sight of the need they have of Christ, and the perfection of His obedience…' (emphasis added throughout).

An Exposition of the Westminster Confession of Faith

We note that God's moral law contains both our duty towards God and our duty to man. In *An Exposition of the Westminster Confession of Faith*, Robert Shaw, a Scottish Presbyterian theologian (1795-1863), writes: 'God having formed man an intelligent creature, and a subject of moral government, he gave him a law for the rule of his conduct. This law was founded in the infinite righteous nature of God, and the moral relations necessarily subsisting between him and man. It was originally written on the heart of man, as he was endowed with such a perfect knowledge of his Maker's will as was sufficient to inform him concerning the whole extent of his duty… *it is also called the moral law*, because it was a revelation of the will of God, as his moral governor, and was the standard and rule of man's moral actions'[8] (emphasis added).

Shaw comments thus on Section 2: 'Upon the fall of man, the law, considered as a covenant of works, was disannulled and set aside; but, *considered as moral, it continued to be a perfect rule of righteousness…* God was graciously pleased to give a new and complete copy of it. He delivered it to the Israelites from Mount Sinai, with awful solemnity…. These commandments were written by the finger of God himself, on two tablets of stone'[9] (emphasis added).

Shaw explains Section 5. The law 'being founded in the relations of men to their Creator, and to one another, it retains its authority under all dispensations. In opposition to the *Antinomians*, who say that believ-ers are released from the obligation of the moral law, our Confession teaches that this law is perpetually binding on justified persons, as well as others. Believers are, indeed, delivered from this law in its covenant form; but they are still under it as a rule of life... Christ, in the most solemn and explicit manner, declared, that he "came not to destroy the law, but to fulfil it" (Matthew 5.17)... The gospel, instead of weakening the obligation of the law, confirms and strengthens its authority, and enforces obedience to its precepts by the strongest motives: "Do we make void the law through faith? God forbid: yea, we establish the law" (Romans 3.31). Although the moral law is to believers divested of its covenant form... it continues in full force as a rule of moral conduct'[10] (emphasis added).

In direct opposition to the antinomians, who say that believers are released from the obligation of the moral law, the Westminster Confession teaches that God's moral law is perpetually binding on all justified persons. And so by Westminster standards, we must conclude that John Piper, who has publicly declared that he is not under the Ten Commandments, is an antinomian. Thus we have the definitive definition he pleaded for in chapter 1.

God's Law Reveals His Character

The moral law is an expression of the character of the True God, who created all things through the power of His Word, and who created man as a moral being in His own image. The Almighty Creator alone has the right and authority to establish the Moral Law of Righteousness whereby all men should live. 'The Law that God placed in the heart of man at creation, and revealed at Mount Sinai, is an expression of His nature. As Creator, God has the right to command His creatures and establish the terms of the relationship between them and Him.'[11]

Scripture teaches that God is holy (Exodus 15.11; Isaiah 6.3), righteous (Psalm 145.17) and good (Psalm 145.9; Luke 18.19); and Scripture also teaches that God's Commandments are holy, and just, and good (Romans 7.12). God is the God of Truth and without iniquity (Deuteronomy 32.4), and all His Commandments are Truth (Psalm 119.142, 151). Our heavenly Father is perfect (Matthew 5.48) and the law of the Lord is perfect, converting the soul (Psalm 19.7). God is love (1 John 4.8), and love is the fulfilling of the law (Romans 13.10). God is Light (1 John 1.5) and the Commandment of God is a lamp and the law is light (Proverbs 6.23). The Lord is pure (1 John 3.3), and the

Commandment of the Lord is pure, enlightening the eyes (Psalm 19.8). God is Spirit and they that worship Him must worship Him in spirit and in truth (John 4.24), and we know that the law is spiritual (Romans 7.14). Scripture teaches that God is immutable: 'For I am the LORD, I change not' (Malachi 3.6); and the law of God is unchanging, 'Till heaven and earth pass, one jot or one tittle shall in no wise pass from the law, till all be fulfilled' (Matthew 5.18). The God of the Bible is 'the LORD, the everlasting God' (Genesis 21.33), and all God's Commandments are sure and stand fast forever and ever (Psalm 111.7-8).

A true believer, who is born of God's Spirit, loves his heavenly Father and delights in His holy law and seeks to obey it.

The New Covenant

The prophet Jeremiah announced the coming of a New Covenant that would supersede the first or Old Covenant, established at Mount Sinai and written on tables of stone. 'But this shall be the covenant that I will make with the house of Israel; After those days, saith the LORD, I will put my law in their inward parts, and write it in their hearts; and will be their God, and they shall be my people' (Jeremiah 31.33). The first Covenant was inadequate—the fault did not lie with God, but with the people who were disobedient. While it set a standard of righteousness, it provided no power to keep it. The New Covenant, ratified by the blood of Christ, deals with man's problem of sin. By His death on the cross, Christ became the Lamb of God, the perfect sacrifice whose blood has the power to wash away sin forever. At the Last Supper our Lord took the cup and said to His disciples: 'For this is my blood of the new testament [covenant], which is shed for many for the remission of sins' (Matthew 26.28). God's grace is fully revealed at Calvary; the free gift of salvation through Christ is available to all who repent of their sins and place their faith in Jesus Christ as Lord and Saviour. The writer of Hebrews reiterates the promise of the New Covenant with regard to the law being written on the hearts of those whose sins God forgives, twice quoting Jeremiah. 'Behold, the days come, saith the Lord, when I will make a new covenant with the house of Israel and with the house of Judah... I will put my laws into their mind, and write them in their hearts: and I will be to them a God, and they shall be to me a people' (Hebrews 8.8, 10).

Under the New Covenant the law is written within the redeemed heart by the regenerating work of the Holy Spirit. Empowered from within by the Holy Spirit, we love the law because we love the Lord. The language of the Christian heart is, 'For I delight in the law of God after the inward man' (Romans 7.22), and, 'O how love I thy law! it is my meditation all the day' (Psalm 119.97). The Westminster Confession expresses this great truth thus: 'the Spirit of Christ subduing and enabling the will of man to do that, freely and cheerfully, which the will of God revealed in the law, requireth to be done' (WCF chapter 19.7).

Christ and the Law

In the Sermon on the Mount the Lord Jesus expands our spiritual understanding of the law. He says: 'Think not that I am come to destroy the law, or the prophets: I am not come to destroy, but to fulfil' (Matthew 5.17). Christ fulfils the law by His perfect, holy life, by His perfect obedience to the law of God, and by His authorative spiritual interpretation of the law.

'For verily I say unto you, Till heaven and earth pass, one jot or one tittle shall in no wise pass from the law, till all be fulfilled' (Matthew 5.18). He restores the true spiritual understanding of the law, which the Pharisees had lost. His teaching is in perfect agreement with the moral commandments of the law and the prophets. The Lord did not come to destroy the law, but to explain it and expand its spiritual application.

He draws a contrast between what the religious leaders had said and what 'He says'. 'Ye have heard that it was said by them of old time, Thou shalt not commit adultery: But I say unto you, That whosoever looketh on a woman to lust after her hath committed adultery with her already in his heart' (Matthew 5.27-28).

Christ gives the true spiritual meaning of the law. The purpose of His mission was not to annul or repeal God's standards of righteousness set out in the law. He did not lessen the law's authority, or free men from the obligation to obey the moral law. So the Lord Jesus did not destroy the law; it stands with all its divine authority. Every human being under heaven is under a lasting obligation to obey it.

'Whosoever therefore shall break one of these least commandments, and shall teach men so, he shall be called the least in the kingdom of heaven: but whosoever shall do and teach them, the same shall be called great in the kingdom of heaven' (Matthew 5.19).

Richard Alderson, in *No Holiness, No Heaven! Antinomianism Today*, comments thus on the moral law: 'God the Creator has imposed His Law on all created beings as the objective expression of His will (Psalm 103.20; Romans 2.15). As Moral Governor of the universe, He is entitled to the unquestioning obedience of all His creatures. Obedience to God (because He is Creator), and to His Moral Law (because it reflects His sovereign will) lies at the heart of all true religion – and thus of sanctification. Becoming a Christian does not alter the fact that I am still a created being under obligation to obey. What conversion does is to enable me to render to God that obedience of which I was incapable as an unbeliever. What is more, it grants me an over-riding desire to obey, since God is now also my Redeemer in Christ Jesus. The Ten Commandments were explicitly applied to God's redeemed people (Exodus 20.1-17). Antinomians have argued that, with the advent of the New Covenant, those commandments lapsed. But this is patently untrue. Our Lord Himself asserted their perpetual validity (Matthew 5.17-18).'[12]

In *The Moral Law*, Dr. Ernest Kevan (1903-1965), Baptist minister, and founder and Principle of London Bible College (now London School of Theology), deals with the abiding validity of the Ten Commandments. He writes: 'In what does sanctified behaviour consist? It consists in pleasing God. What is it that pleases God? The doing of His will. Where is His will to be discerned? In His holy Law. The Law, then, is the Christian's rule of life, and the believer finds that he delights in the Law of God after the inward man (Romans 7.22). The Christian is not lawless but "under the law to Christ", a phrase from Paul which would be more accurately rendered "in the law of Christ" (1 Corinthians 9.21)… The Law of God, therefore, not only instructs the believer in that kind of life which is well-pleasing to God, but is the humbling instrument by which the Holy Spirit leads the believer to discover his shortcomings, to grieve over them, to repent of them, and so to apply himself to the Lord Jesus Christ in whom alone the grace of sanctification is found.'[13]

Piper and the Ten Commandments

We can now begin to understand the significance of Piper's position on the moral law. In chapter 1, we heard him say that Christians are not under the Ten Commandments and then allude to the second half of Romans 6.14, 'The Bible says we're not under the law', omitting the first part of the verse, 'For sin shall not have dominion over you'. We also heard him demean the Ten Commandments with patronising praise—'The Ten Commandments are really important, you should hang them on your wall and you should measure your life by them, but in a very different way than when you were under them, because they have been kept for you.' Piper also said: 'We are acceptable in Christ, which puts commandment-keeping at a lower level—the way to live the Christian life is not by focusing on commandments...' Piper provocatively described the Ten Commandments as a 'list' that believers keep in their 'pocket'. So while paying lip-service to the Ten Commandments, Piper teaches Christians that they are *no longer under them*, and therefore should *put commandment-keeping at a lower level*. The essence of Piper's teaching is that obedience to God's moral law is not really important.

With this understanding of antinomianism and of God's moral law established in our minds, we are now in a position to evaluate Piper's teaching in the light of Scripture. We shall examine three of Piper's addresses, which have been recorded and placed in the public domain as YouTube videos. The first video is, 'The Origin of the Unwasted Life'. The second video is, 'Jesus Saves from Morality', which is an extract from Piper's talk, 'Lessons from an Inconsolable Soul: Learning from the Mind and Heart of C. S. Lewis'. The third video is, 'The Ultimate Essence of Evil', abstracted from Piper's talk to Passion 2017. In each video Piper clearly reveals his antinomian mindset.

Endnotes

1. Mark Jones, *Antinomianism: Reformed Theology's Unwelcome Guest?*, P&R Publishing, 2013, p125
2. http://www.limerickreformed.com/blog/2013/08/03/belgic-confession-article-25-the-abolishing-of-the-ceremonial-law

3. The Reformation Bible Study, 'The Threefold Use of the Law', from Nathan W. Bingham, http://www.ligonier.org/blog/threefold-use-law/

4. John Calvin, 'How Do Believers Have Need of the Law - The Third and Principle Use', based on *Calvin's Institutes*, 2.7.12, https://www.mon-ergism.com/how-do-believers-have-need-law-third-and-principle-use,

5. Ibid, based on *Calvin's Institutes*, 2.7.12, 13

6. *Instruction in Christianity*, J.P. Wiles, A Summary of Calvin's Institutes, Sovereign Grace Union, 1920, 1966, Book 2, chapters 7 and 8, pp107-109

7. 'William Tyndale and the Politics of Grace 1'. The Rev. Dr Simon Oliver, University of Wales. A paper given at the Fourth Oxford Tyndale Conference, Hertford College, Oxford September 2005. http://www.tyndale.org/tsj30/oliver.htm

8. Robert Shaw, *An exposition of the Westminster Confession of Faith*, 1845, Christian Focus Publications, 1998 edition, p240

9. Ibid, pp241-242

10. Ibid, p245

11. Ernest Reisinger, *The Law and the Gospel*, P&R Publishing, 1997, p12

12. Richard Alderson, *No Holiness, No Heaven! Antinomianism Today*, Banner of Truth, 1986, pp20-21

13. Ernest Kevan, *The Moral Law*, Sovereign Grace Publishers, 2001, pp1-2

Chapter 4

The Unwasted Life

Our first example is an excerpt from John Piper's address entitled, 'The Origin of the Unwasted Life', given to the Desiring God Regional Conference in March 2008.[1] He describes the 'Unwasted Life' as a life in which Christ is magnified by our cherishing Him and valuing Him above all things. The problem, according to Piper, is 'we are not a people who by nature treasure Christ above all things'. He then asks the question: 'What's the nature of our depravity—sin, fallenness, corruption? What is the nature of all your depravity? What's the essence of it? Let me give you a sentence which I think is the essence of my depravity, and yours, my corruption, my fallenness, my sin, that has to be fixed. I can't fix it; it has to be fixed for me. Here's my definition of what's wrong with you, and me and everybody in the world.'

Piper continues: 'The inner essence of our depravity is our *preferring* – very important word – our *preferring* the glory of created things over the glory of God and Christ. Our preferring the joy, pleasure, delight, beauty, attractiveness, satisfying nature of created reality over Creator, God and His Son. We *prefer* His gifts over Him, that's the essence of our wickedness' (Piper's emphasis).

Law-Breaking not the Main Problem

Piper elaborates: 'Now why do I define depravity that way? Why not define depravity in terms of *law-breaking*? I sort of grew up this way. God has a law: Don't eat this tree. You break the law by eating the tree. God punishes you with judgement. You must find deliverance from that judgement. That's the paradigm I grew up with, and the reason I'm not talking that way is because it is so non-penetrating to your soul's need. Law-breaking is *not* your main problem!' (Piper's emphasis).

Piper's Caricature

Here we note how Piper has created a caricature of the orthodox view of the Fall. As he rejects the 'paradigm' that God punishes law-breaking, he is able to say, 'law-breaking is *not* your main problem'. But he is distorting Scripture, which makes it clear that Adam and Eve *rebelled* against God's *command* regarding the tree of the knowledge of good and evil: 'thou shalt not eat of it: for in the day that thou eatest thereof thou shalt surely die' (Genesis 2.17). They disobeyed this very first commandment and stood guilty before God as lawbreakers. But Piper rejects the idea of punishment and judgement as 'non-penetrating' to the soul. He wants a gospel that downplays judgement and the consequences of disobeying God's law, replacing it with a gospel that 'prefers' God above all things.

Scripture declares that God is the Judge of all the earth (Genesis 18.25), and all men and women will stand before the Judgement Seat to give an account of how they kept God's holy law. The gospel of grace offers the hope of forgiveness and new life in Christ to all who repent of their sin and turn in faith to the Saviour, who died for sin on the Cross of Calvary. The believer, the one who is justified by faith in Christ, is cleansed from all sin by the blood of Christ. This is the real message of the gospel, which is indeed deeply penetrating (to use Piper's word) to the soul of every sinner to whom the Holy Spirit reveals the truth of the gospel.

Piper gives several reasons for his statement, 'Law-breaking is *not* your main problem'. He says: 'Number one: the first commandment of the law is "You shall love", and immediately people get nervous and they reduce it to actions. They say: "Love is obedience – love is obedience", because they don't want the heart to be impugned at that moment. I'm not mainly interested in whether you *break laws*, I'm mainly interested in whether you love God or not, or love His stuff' (Piper's emphasis).

He continues: 'Jesus said on this point, John 14.15, "If you love me you will keep my commandments"—that does not mean that love me equals keep my commandments. It emphatically means the opposite, namely, love must exist and out of that love will come obedience to my commandments; they're not the same, otherwise the sentence makes no sense. If you love me, that's one thing, you will obey me, that's a second thing. And this is the problem, *this is secondary*— I want to go to the heart of my problem, I don't want to dink around here at the edges where I would perform, got to perform better. I want to know what's wrong here [pointing to his chest]. Why do I get up leaning away from God in the morning?' (Piper's emphasis).

Piper has just said that obedience to God is a secondary thing—but such teaching is deeply heretical. As we have seen, God gave Adam a specific command not to eat of the fruit from the tree of knowledge of good and evil. Adam knew what God had said but chose to disobey. *Adam's transgression was to violate God's command.* By this act of disobedience sin was introduced into the world and with it the penalty for sin, which is death. Adam and Eve were expelled from the Garden of Eden for disobeying God's commandment. 'For as by one man's disobedience many were made sinners…' (Romans 5.19). The man who says he loves God, but disobeys His commandments is a liar and a hypocrite (1 John 2.4). Piper's assertion that obedience is a secondary thing (plausible as he tries to make it sound) is a sure sign of his antinomianism. 'And hereby do we know that we know him, if we keep his commandments' (1 John 2.3).

Doing the Law Begrudgingly

Piper continues: 'Here's a second reason I talk this way, because *laws can be broken by doing them begrudgingly.* By doing them, *laws can be broken by doing them*—laws can be broken by doing them—begrudgingly. I get that from 1 John 5.3. "This is the love of God, that we keep his commandments. And his commandments are not burdensome." If you do His commandments, "Ah, I hate these commandments, but you have to do them, so I am going to do them, because I want to be known as a lover of God." That's ridiculous' (Piper's emphasis).

Piper goes on: 'Loving God is such a profound transformation of what you *prefer*, that the burden is lifted. "Come unto me all you who labour and are heavy laden and I will give you rest. Take my yoke upon you and learn from me, for I am meek and lowly in heart and you will find rest for the soul." The yoke goes on, and rest happens, because you love Him, He satisfies… *So I'm not talking about law-breaking when I define my depravity*, mainly because I can do these laws begrudgingly and it's no sign of love to God' (Piper's emphasis).

Preferring God

We have heard Piper describe the believer's relationship with God as a 'preferring' relationship. He defines the 'Unwasted Life' as one that *prefers* Christ above all else.

'Prefer' is defined as an action taken to *promote* one thing over another, to *like* something as better, or *to give priority* to one thing over another. To promote, to like, to give priority are voluntary actions taken by man when he considers a number of options. To 'prefer' is therefore to make a voluntary choice. In using this term in reference to the salvation of man, Piper is effectively offering a salvation by voluntary choice rather than a salvation by the grace of God.

From Scripture we know this is not possible. 'But the natural man receiveth not the things of the Spirit of God: for they are foolishness unto him: neither can he know them, because they are spiritually discerned' (1 Corinthians 2.14). Natural man, in and of himself, cannot and does not voluntarily choose or prefer God over other options—'There is none that understandeth, there is none that seeketh after God' (Romans 3.11). For Piper to teach that we should develop a 'preference' for God is presenting us with an impossible task.

It is God who chooses man. It is God who 'prefers' man, not the other way round. A Christian is one who is 'born not of blood, nor of the will of the flesh, nor of the will of man, but of God' (John 1.13). The Lord said to His disciples: 'Ye have not chosen me, but I have chosen you' (John 15.16).

Although Piper says we do not 'treasure' Christ by nature, to use terminology that conveys the notion of salvation as a voluntary choice on the part of man is a serious misrepresentation of the gospel, which leads unwitting listeners to trust in their own ability to 'prefer' God, when Scripture warns that 'there is none that seeketh after God' (Romans 3.11).

Equally troubling is his advocacy of personal pleasure as the ultimate motivation behind our 'preference' for God. The very use of the term 'treasuring' Christ above all things not only conveys the same voluntary action inherent in the word 'preferring', it also establishes maximum personal pleasure as the fundamental motivation for man to choose God over created things. Piper's hedonistic approach to salvation should not surprise us, for it has been the hallmark of his Desiring

God ministry for over thirty years. Piper writes: 'Unless a man be born again into a Christian Hedonist he cannot see the kingdom of God.'[2] Elsewhere he says, 'The pursuit of pleasure is an essential motive for every good deed. If you abandon the pursuit of full and lasting pleasure, you cannot love people or please God.'[3] Such an assertion contradicts Scripture: 'Love seeketh not her own' (1 Corinthians 13.5). Christian Hedonism, which is the central teaching of Piper's ministry, is predicated on antinomianism.

The Essence of Human Sin

Piper's error starts with his wrong view of the Fall of man. He locates the Fall of man at the point where he 'preferred' the creature over the Creator, and defines 'the essence of our wickedness' as continuing with this 'preferring'. The solution Piper offers to fallen man, dead in his trespasses and sins (Ephesians 2.1), is to 'prefer' God above all things. Piper says the essence of human sin and depravity is not law-breaking; rather the essence of human sin is 'preferring' other things above God. At the Desiring God 2015 Conference for Pastors, in the Minneapolis Convention Center, Piper said the root of all sinning is 'a heart that prefers anything above God, a heart that does not treasure God over all other persons and all other things.'[4] In his address at the Passion Conference 2017 (discussed in chapter 6), Piper said: 'The ultimate essence of evil is the loss of taste for God as our all-satisfying life and joy, and the *preference* for other things above God himself.'[5] So in Piper's mind sin is essentially a wrong preference, not the breaking of the moral law.

The apostle Paul, in dealing with sin, does not express himself in Piper's terms of a wrong preference. In Romans chapter 5, Paul, in explaining the cause of the Fall, speaks of the breaking of God's first commandment to humanity (Genesis 2.17). Robert Shaw explains that God's first commandment was a test of *obedience*. 'Their [Adam and Eve] abstaining from the tree of knowledge was the criterion by which their fidelity was to be tried, and their eating of the fruit of that tree was a violation of the whole law: for it was rebellion against the Lawgiver, and a renunciation of his authority.'[6] Paul interprets the Fall thus: 'For as by one man's *disobedience* [Adam] many were made sinners, so by the *obedience* of one [Christ] shall many be made righteous'

(Romans 5.19). The apostle does not delve 'behind' this law-breaking to identify a more fundamental paradigm of 'preference' for things other than God. Scripture is clear—God demands obedience to His commandments: 'But this thing commanded I them, saying, Obey my voice, and I will be your God, and ye shall be my people: and walk ye in all the ways that I have commanded you, that it may be well unto you' (Jeremiah 7.23). Behind Piper's failure to understand these great truths is his antinomian determination to eliminate law-keeping as an essential element of the Christian way of life.

While Piper defines sin *subjectively* as a *preference*, the Bible defines sin *objectively* as *transgression* of the law (1 John 3.4) and states that 'all unrighteousness is sin' (1 John 5.17). Rebellion against God's Word lies at the heart of all sin. Piper says the reason he rejects the orthodox understanding of the Fall is because 'it is so non-penetrating to your soul's need'. God the Creator gave mankind a clear and unambiguous law—'But of the tree of the knowledge of good and evil, thou shalt not eat of it'—and Piper says it can be disregarded. Because he does not regard the first commandment of God as important he is able to say, 'Law-breaking is not your main problem!' Such a statement is blatant antinomianism.

Downplaying Law-keeping

Piper says the first commandment of the law is 'You shall love', and then says, 'I'm not mainly interested in whether you break laws, I'm mainly interested in whether you love God or not, or love His stuff.'

Here we discern another major error in Piper's teaching. While he teaches that we must love God, he does not teach that we must keep God's law. He says he is not mainly interested in whether we keep God's law, clearly implying it is of less importance. The apostle John says that the person who claims to be Christian and does not keep Christ's commandments is a liar. 'He that saith, I know him, and keepeth not his commandments, is a liar, and the truth is not in him' (1 John 2.4). What does this verse of Scripture say about a Christian minister who is not interested in teaching his flock to keep God's Commandments? Piper says the reason he talks like this about breaking laws is 'because laws can be broken by doing them begrudgingly'.

Here he is presenting a distorted view of the Christian life, inferring that believers actually dislike the Commandments of God and find them such a burden that they only reluctantly keep them. But this is a travesty, for real born-again Christians delight in the law of God (Romans 7.22), which is holy, just and good (Romans 7.12). And their greatest burden is not carnal reluctance, but the daily struggle against indwelling sin. A true child of God delights in God's law yet agonises over his failure to keep it. 'For I delight in the law of God after the inward man: but I see another law in my members, warring against the law of my mind, and bringing me into captivity to the law of sin which is in my members' (Romans 7.22-23). Piper's comments reveal a mindset that is deeply hostile to God's moral law, and shockingly at variance with God's Word.

Piper again: 'So I'm not talking about law-breaking when I define my depravity, mainly because I can do these laws begrudgingly and it's no sign of love to God.' No indeed! The man who says he keeps God's law and has resentment in his heart is breaking God's law. Such a man is not a true believer, but a hypocrite. A man who loves God seeks to obey His Commandments and does so with a joyful heart. Again Piper has made his antinomianism obvious. At the centre of his Christian Hedonism is the preference for pleasure in God before obedience to Him, and this marks out Piper as antinomian.

Endnotes

1. Desiring God website, Piper address 'The Origin of the Unwasted Life' at Desiring God 2008 Regional Conference, March 2008, http://www.desiringgod.org/messages/the-origin-of-the-unwasted-life
2. John Piper, *Desiring God*, Multinomah, 2011, p55
3. Desiring God website, transcript of Piper's sermon, 'Love: The Labor of Christian Hedonism', October 1983, https://www.desiringgod.org/messages/love-the-labor-of-christian-hedonism
4. Desiring God website, Piper's address, 'What Is Sin? The Essence and Root of All Sinning', Plenary Session – 2015 Conference for Pastors, February 2015, https://www.desiringgod.org/messages/the-origin-essence-and-definition-of-sin'

5. Piper's address to Passion Conference 2017, 'The Ultimate Essence of Evil, The Majesty of God, the Triumph of Christ, and the Glory of Human Life', https://www.desiringgod.org/messages/the-ultimate-essence-of-evil

6. Robert Shaw, *An exposition of the Westminster Confession of Faith*, 1845, Christian Focus Publications, 1998 edition, p112

Chapter 5

Piper Smites Morality

Our second example is from a John Piper address to the Desiring God 2010 Conference for Pastors entitled, 'Lessons from an Inconsolable Soul: Learning from the Mind and Heart of C.S. Lewis'. Piper's Desiring God organisation published a short extract from this address in a five-minute YouTube video entitled, 'Jesus Saves from Morality'. This chapter is based on these two sources. In his address Piper asked: 'Why has he [Lewis] been so significant for me, even though he is not Reformed in his doctrine, and could barely be called an evangelical by typical American uses of that word?'[1]

Piper concedes that 'Lewis does not believe in the inerrancy of Scripture... He doesn't treat the Reformation with respect, but thinks it could have been avoided, and calls aspects of it farcical.' But there is more. Undoubtedly Lewis was heavily influenced by Roman Catholics, such as J. R. R. Tolkien and G. K. Chesterton, and so closely aligned with Catholic theology that 'many who read Lewis's first book after his conversion, *The Pilgrim's Regress*, assumed he was a Catholic, and, in fact, the second edition was published by a Catholic publisher.'[2] Today he continues to be accepted by Rome as much as he is by evangelicals.[3] An article in the *Catholic Herald* (2013) entitled, 'C. S. Lewis came so close to Catholicism', refers to Lewis's dislike of 'Protestant fundamentalism', and says that 'his aim was always to help the cause of reunion or at least make it clear why we ought to be reunited'.[4]

What was it about the work of this universally admired man that Piper found so helpful? The answer, according to Piper, 'lies in the way that the experience of joy and the defence of truth come together in Lewis's life and writings'. But, as we shall see in this chapter, it was Lewis's antinomian tendencies that really attracted Piper.

The Abolition of Man

In discussing what he regards as the virtues of Lewis, Piper mentions the book, *The Abolition of Man* (1944), in which Lewis argues against those who trivialise truth and beauty into mere personal preference and subjectivity. Lewis's concern is that, as a consequence of such a philosophy, there will be no resistance to tyrants who simply declare themselves to be in the right. Against what he regards as a suicidal view of truth and reality, he defends his version of absolute Truth and absolute Value.

The Abolition of Man is an important book because it tells us much about Lewis's view of truth and of morality. In an appendix he published a list of what he regarded as universal moral principles, which he calls 'Illustrations of the Tao or Natural Law'. His list of 'moral principles' is made up of quotes from Christian, Jewish, Egyptian, Babylonian, Roman, Old Norse, Greek, Hindu, Australian Aborigine, Chinese, and American Indian sources. Lewis's understanding of the *Tao* also includes five of the Ten Commandments from the Christian Bible: Honour your father and your mother; You shall not murder; You shall not commit adultery; You shall not steal; You shall not give false testimony against your neighbour. The other five Commandments, four of which deal with man's duty to God, don't make it on to Lewis's illustrative list.

Dr Gary Greg, who holds the Mitch McConnell Chair in Leadership at the University of Louisville, USA, comments: 'In his 1944 book *The Abolition of Man*, Lewis wrote in support of the great moral tradition that unites nearly all of humanity who seek wisdom in ancient texts and modes of life. We have a choice, he argued, of either being part of this great tradition that he called "The Tao" (or "The Way") or we can be outside all legitimate claims of morality. Morality is to be found, not created, he taught… It is modern man, scientific and materialist man, who seeks to break the cake of old morality to fit his new ambitions rather than to make his ambitions fit within the larger scheme of natural law that unites so much of the Jewish, Christian, Buddhist, Confucionist, Roman, Greek and pagan traditions.'[5]

The audio transcript of Piper's address quotes from *The Abolition of Man*:

> This thing which I [Lewis] have called for convenience the
> *Tao*, and which others may call Natural Law or Traditional

> Morality… is not one among a series of possible systems of value. It is the *sole source* of all value judgements. If it is rejected, all value is rejected… The rebellion of new ideologies against the *Tao* is a rebellion of the branches against the tree: if the rebels could succeed they would find that they had destroyed themselves.

Here we must note that Lewis regards the *Tao* as the *sole source* of all value judgements. Obviously Lewis was not a practising Taoist (an ancient Chinese religion); but he borrows the term *Tao* – meaning 'The Way' – as shorthand for his concept of universal moral principles that have an objective reality. For a Christian to use the term, however, is unfortunate. What is really worrying is that Lewis calls the *Tao* the sole source of all value judgements. Where does that leave the Bible?

Interpreting C.S. Lewis

There is no doubt that Lewis was not a friend of Reformed Christianity. His sympathies were definitely with Catholic spirituality, although he always remained within the pale of the Church of England as an Anglo-Catholic. He had a profound dislike for the Protestant faith. He did not believe in the inerrancy of Scripture. The fact that Lewis published a list of what he regarded as universal moral principles derived from non-Christian sources, including five of the Ten Commandments, and the 'wisdom' of pagan gods, raises a number of disturbing questions about Lewis's version of 'mere' Christianity. That his list included statements from a number of other 'gods' suggests that he did not regard the Ten Commandments as the unique moral law of God for all people for all time. And so we must ask, what moral standard guides the views of Lewis and his admirer John Piper? If indeed they live by the 'wisdom' of the *Tao*, what is their position with regard to the third use of the law? And if the *Tao* is 'The Way', was Christ wrong when He said, 'I am the Way, the Truth, and the Life'? (John 14.6).

Jesus Saves from Morality

With this background we turn to the audio transcript of Piper's video labelled, 'Jesus saves from Morality'.[6] Piper says: 'Until we are gripped with joyful impulses of the gospel — joyful inner impulses of the gospel of grace, from the inside — until we're gripped by that, we're always thinking in terms of doing external duties with pressures from outside. "Here's the list of stuff to do. God will be pleased if we do it, and now we're going to work up the will power to do it." That's just religion. That's religion, that's morality. C.S. Lewis is massively penetrating and insightful at this point. Listen to these two quotes [from Lewis]:

> A perfect man would never act from a sense of duty. He'd always want the right thing more than the wrong one. Duty is only a substitute for love of God or of other people. Like a crutch, which is a substitute for a leg. Most of us need the crutch at times, but of course, it's idiotic to use the crutch when our legs, our own loves and tastes and habits, can do the journey on their own. A perfect man would never act from duty.

[Piper continues] 'Now, the pursuit of holiness, therefore, is transformed. My teaching on sanctification is transformed. Some of you come from traditions in which this — what I'm saying right now — is just totally, utterly unknown. Unknown. Everything is lists. Conformity to external pressures in the church. You gotta dress a certain way, talk a certain way, do stuff. C.S. Lewis is saying no good man acts that way. You say, "Wait a minute. We built a whole church around that!"'

[Piper again] 'Now, here's the really profound thing. This next quote [from Lewis], this is the one from the *Oxford History of English Literature*. It's about the Reformation, it's about Puritans, and it's about William Tyndale in particular. What was William Tyndale about? What were the Protestant Reformers about? Listen to this:

> In reality, Tyndale is trying to express an obstinate fact which meets us long before we venture into the realm of theology: the fact that morality or duty (what he calls the Law) never yet made a man happy in himself or dear to others. It is shocking, but it is undeniable. We do not wish either to be or to live among people who are clean, or honest, or kind as a matter of duty. We want to be and associate with people who like being clean and honest and kind. The mere suspicion that what seemed an act of spontaneous friendliness or generosity was really done as a duty, subtly poisons it. In philosophical language, the ethical category is "self-destructive." Morality is healthy only when

it is trying to abolish itself. In theological language, no man can be saved by works. The whole purpose of the gospel for Tyndale is to deliver us from morality. Thus, paradoxically, the Puritan of modern imagination, the cold, gloomy heart doing as duty what happier and richer souls do without thinking of it, is precisely the enemy which historical Protestantism arose and smote.

[Piper] 'That's powerful. That's powerful. I just want to *keep smiting*, that's what Christian Hedonism is. It's the *smite on morality*. It's the *smite on religion*. It's the *smite* on externality and performance, and *laws and lists* that don't come from in here [pointing to his heart]. That have never tasted the joy, that have never embraced the absolute rock-solid, heart-enlivening truth. We're at war, that's what Christianity is in my judgment' (Piper's emphasis).

Lewis's use of Tyndale as an example of a man who wants to 'deliver us from morality' is wide of the mark. Tyndale's passion was to deliver his countrymen from the Roman Catholic bondage of law-keeping as a way of salvation. He believed in a salvation through faith in Christ which enables born-again believers to obey God's moral law from a regenerated heart as an act of joyful duty.

As we evaluate Piper's teaching in the 'Jesus Saves from Morality' video, we need to be aware of Lewis's influence on Piper's ministry. Orthodox Christianity believes that true morality is that which conforms to God's moral law, and immoral conduct is that which breaks God's moral law. So a Christian distinguishes right from wrong by reference to God's moral law and rejects the Natural Law or morality of Lewis's *Tao*. But Piper quotes Lewis on morality with uncritical enthusiasm.

Interpreting Piper

In this video Piper distinguishes between, on the one hand, 'joyful inner impulses' that come from inside, and on the other hand, 'external duties' from outside, characterised by a 'list of stuff to do'. Here we should remind ourselves that in chapter 1 he mockingly refers to the Ten Commandments as a *list* we keep in our pocket. Piper is concerned that Christians are always thinking in terms of doing external duties, like doing a *list* of things that please God. Instead of obeying the external *list* of stuff, he wants Christians to be gripped by joyful inner impulses that come from inside. So Piper has skilfully created a false dichotomy between two approaches to Christian living—one approach is to obey an external list of things (which we identify in the next paragraph as the Ten Commandments); the other is to follow the joyful inner impulses from inside.

Laws and Lists

Piper is concerned that Christians are always thinking in terms of doing external duties: 'Here's the list of stuff to do. God will be pleased if we do it, and now we're going to work up the will power to do it. That's just religion. That's religion, that's morality.' What does Piper have in mind when he refers to a list of stuff? It is not difficult to discern that the 'list of stuff' is Piper's code for the Ten Commandments. Note also Piper's suggestion that those Christians who are seeking to please God by obeying His moral law, need to work up their will power. But the Psalmist joyfully declares: 'I delight to do thy will, O my God: yea, thy law is within my heart' (Psalm 40.8) and, 'O how love I thy law! it is my meditation all the day' (Psalm 119.97). Clearly, believers, who have the law of God within their hearts, do not need to work up their will power to obey it; they are enabled by the indwelling Holy Spirit. Piper seems to be unaware that the law of God is within the heart of the believer. Believers do not think of obeying God's law as an external duty, but as a spiritual duty, pleasing to their heavenly Father.

Inner Impulses of the Heart

Having warned Christians of the dangers of following 'laws and lists', Piper wants them to be gripped by what he refers to as the joyful inner impulses from inside, that is, the heart. Although he qualifies this with the phrase 'of the gospel', he gives no warning of the dangers inherent in following the human heart, even if it is regenerate. Here we should note the warning of Scripture: 'The heart is deceitful above all things, and desperately wicked: who can know it?' (Jeremiah 17.9). The heart is virtually unsearchable to human beings. Certainly no one can fully understand the heart of man. Jeremiah speaks of the deceitfulness in a man's heart toward himself. A fundamental biblical truth is that the heart of all people, even true believers, is tainted by sin. Our Lord said, out of the heart come evil ideas, murder, adultery, sexual immorality, theft, lies, slander (Matthew 15.18-20). And Piper wants us to follow the inner impulses of our heart!

Piper is adamant that he is at 'war' with 'morality'. His zeal knows no bounds—'I just want to keep smiting, that's what Christian Hedonism is. It's the smite on morality.' Here we see the picture of a dedicated antinomian who is seeking to replace biblical morality and duty with some ill-defined spiritual instinct, located in his heart. And he is encouraging others to do the same. When he refers to his teaching on sanctification, he makes it clear that it is not based on 'laws and lists'. In other words, his teaching on sanctification rejects God's moral law—he rejects the third use of the law as a rule of life for Christians. So when he declares that his teaching on sanctification is not based on 'laws and lists', he is declaring himself to be an antinomian.

Piper takes delight in quoting Lewis's opinion that 'morality is healthy only when it is trying to abolish itself'. Clearly, Lewis and Piper do not like biblical morality and neither do they like duty. Why is this so? Is it because they both have abrogated God's moral law in their thinking? Indeed, at the beginning of this study we heard Piper say that he is not under the law; and we know Lewis advocated the impersonal *Tao* as the *sole source* of universal morality.

Duty

'A perfect man would never act from a sense of duty. He'd always want the right thing more than the wrong one.' Lewis and Piper, in their discussion of duty, avoid reference to the biblical view, namely, that the whole duty of man is to fear God and obey His Commandments (Ecclesiastes 12.13). They fail to mention that the first four Commandments outline man's duty to God and the last six Commandments man's duty to man. But this is no surprise, for the first four Commandments do not make it onto Lewis's illustrative list of the *Tao*.

Instead, these men seek to create the impression that there is something not quite right with acting out of a sense of duty. The perfect man is the one who wants to do the right thing, whereas the imperfect man needs the threat imposed by duty to coerce him into doing the right thing. In this way duty is downgraded as a biblical virtue. But Lewis's teaching, so admired by Piper, is misleading. Where is this perfect man? Only Christ was perfect, and in loving duty as the Representative Man (that is, the Last Adam) He obeyed his Father perfectly on our behalf. The apostle Paul emphasised the struggle a Christian has with sin: 'For I know that in me (that is, in my flesh,) dwelleth no good thing: for to will is present with me; but how to perform that which is good I find not. For the good that I would I do not: but the evil which I would not, that I do... O wretched man that I am! who shall deliver me from the body of this death?' (Romans 7.18-19, 24).

Paul loved God's moral law (Romans 7.22), as do all true believers. His experience was ours, however: 'But I see another law in my members, warring against the law of my mind, and bringing me into captivity to the law of sin which is in my members' (Romans 7.23). There is no such thing as a perfect man who always wants to do the right thing this side of eternity. All believers struggle against indwelling sin and long to do better. We desire to obey God out of loving duty. So duty is not antithetical to loving God and obeying Him.

Piper has called on Lewis to buttress his antinomian stance. But Lewis's universal Natural Law, expressed in the *Tao*, conveniently waters down God's moral law, expressed in the Ten Commandments. And lying deeper than the antinomianism is Piper's commitment to Christian Hedonism—the Christian life predicated on taking pleasure in God while ignoring the duty to obey God's moral law.

Endnotes

1. Desiring God website, Piper's address, 'Lessons from an Inconsolable Soul: Learning from the Mind and Heart of C.S. Lewis', Desiring God 2010 Conference for Pastors, 2 February 2010, https://www.desiringgod. org/messages/lessons-from-an-inconsolable-soul

2. Think on These Things website, article 'C S Lewis' by Gary Gilley, (September 2006 – Volume 12, Issue 8), Think on These Things Ministries is a vital outreach ministry of Southern View Chapel. http://tottministries.org/cs-lewis/

3. Ibid

4. Catholic Herald, 'C S Lewis came so close to Catholicism', by Mary Forster posted Friday, 22 Nov 2013, http://www.catholicherald.co.uk/news/2013/11/22/c-s-lewis-came-so-close-to-catholicism/

5. Dr Gary Greg, The Dalai, the Dinosaur, and the Tao, http://www.theimaginativeconservative.org/2013/05/the-dalai-the-tao-cs-lewis.html

6. YouTube video, Jesus Saves from Morality, May 8 2017, http://www.desiringgod.org/messages/lessons-from-an-inconsolable-soul/excerpts/jesus-saves-from-morality

Chapter 6

Passion Conference 2017

Our final example is from John Piper's address to Passion 2017 in Atlanta, Georgia, entitled, 'The Ultimate Essence of Evil'.[1] In his talk Piper openly reveals his antinomian opposition to law-keeping. He first describes what he understands to be the ultimate essence of evil. He says that losing a taste for God, or preferring anything or anybody more than God, is the ultimate essence of evil. To quote Piper's words: 'The ultimate essence of evil is a preference for other things, other people, anything created more than God, that's the ultimate essence of evil, biblically.' To emphasise his point he boldly declares: 'Disobedience or law-breaking is *not* the ultimate essence of evil.' And, 'the ultimate essence of evil is the failure to be satisfied in God'. He also downplays the evil of rebellion, making it a lesser evil than losing 'a taste for God'.

The Fall of Man

Piper explains to his large audience of mainly young people the ultimate essence of the first, original, world-infecting sin. He reads Genesis 3.1-6, and then quotes Romans 5.12 and says: 'Sin came into the world through one man, and death through sin, and so death spread to billions and billions and billions of people over the thousands of years of human history. You came into the world totally captive to this sin. What's the essence of it? What's the ultimate essence of the first, original, world-infecting sin?' He says that when Eve saw that the forbidden fruit was good for food, a delight to the eyes and desirable to make one wise, she reasoned that God wanted to keep it from her. So she took and ate and gave it to her husband. 'We will not be denied what we desire more than God.' Piper asks, 'What was the essence of the fall of humanity? Was it the eating of the forbidden fruit? No!' He says: 'The moral outrage, the horror of what happened here was that Adam and Eve *desired, desired, desired* this fruit more than God.

That's the essence of evil... eating was not the essence of evil, because before they ate they had lost their taste for God, and that's the ultimate outrage in the universe' (Piper's emphasis). He adamantly rejects the idea that rebellion against God's authority is more primal than desiring something above God. He openly declares: 'Disobedience to the command of God is not more basic, not more fundamental than what they [Adam and Eve] desired above God.'

But Piper has failed to put his interpretation of the Fall into a proper biblical context, for he did not remind his young audience that God *commanded* Adam not to eat of the tree of the knowledge of good and evil. In an act of wilful disobedience, Adam and Eve *rebelled* against the *commandment* of God.

Clearly in God's eyes the sin of Adam and Eve was *disobedience* to His command 'thou shalt not eat of it'. But Piper sees things differently; he answers his question about rebellion against God's authority thus: 'I've been taught they disobeyed. Period.' And then from Piper comes an emphatic No! 'Disobedience to the command of God is not more basic, not more fundamental, not more ultimate than what they desired above God.' Piper's interpretation of the sin of Adam and Eve is unbiblical and misleading. But as we saw in chapter 4, the apostle Paul is clear: 'For as by one man's disobedience [Adam] many were made sinners, so by the obedience of one [Christ] shall many be made righteous' (Romans 5.19). Paul makes no reference to a *prior* preferring of anything to God. And the Westminster Shorter Catechism, Question 39, teaches: 'The duty which God requireth of man is *obedience* to his revealed will' (emphasis added). We appreciate that sin always begins in the thought life, but even then it is disobedience and rebellion. Piper's thesis is that preferring comes before disobedience. This stance is vital to his doctrine of Christian Hedonism, where preferring God leads to obedience. But such thinking is antinomian and unbiblical. Indeed, the final chapter in the last book in the Bible emphasises the importance of obeying God: 'Blessed are they that do his commandments, that they may have right to the tree of life, and may enter in through the gates into the city' (Revelation 22.14). Here we see the primal disobedience in the Garden gloriously reversed in the gospel, where our ability to obey is restored.

Piper's false dichotomy

To emphasise his message that commandment-keeping is not the important thing, Piper goes on to present his audience with a choice between
two alternatives. He says with emphasis, 'Obedience to God's Commandments, delight in God's character, have you got those two? Which
of these is more essential?' Piper is trying to force his audience to choose
between obedience to God's Commandments on the one hand and delight
in God's character on the other hand—and to make one more essential
and so the other less essential. His aim is to convince his audience that
'delight in God' stands above 'obedience to God's Commandments'.
But Piper has created a false dichotomy, for the two options are not
mutually exclusive, but intimately related. Therefore to be asked to
choose between them is illegitimate. Christians who delight in God's
character are also those who seek to obey His Commandments, which
reveal God's loving, holy, righteous character. Piper's false dichotomy
is disingenuous, for it is forcing believers to choose between two essential truths. Such a thing is both theologically wrong and pastorally
dangerous —it misleads God's people, especially the young.

Rebellion

Piper deals with the issue of rebellion thus: 'But someone might ask:
Isn't rebellion against God's authority a deeper, more primal problem
than the heart's preference for the fruit? Isn't disobedience the real issue,
the deepest essence of evil? No. And the reason I stress this is because
as long as you see *commandment-keeping* as the essence of good, and
commandment-breaking as the essence of evil, you will never get to
the bottom of why you do what you do, or are what you are. You will
never see the greatness of God's majesty, or the fullness of Christ's triumph, or the beauty of a life that pleases God if you think the essence
of evil is commandment-breaking' (Piper's emphasis). In other words,
in order to see the greatness of God's majesty and the beauty of a life
that pleases God, you need to free yourself from the idea that it is right
to obey God by keeping His Commandments. This is antinomianism
disguised as pleasing God.

Piper is saying that if we believe that obedience to God's Commandments is at the centre of a life that is pleasing to God, then we are

sadly mistaken. And if we see disobedience (commandment-breaking) as the essence of a life that is displeasing to God, then we have deluded ourselves and are without spiritual understanding, and know nothing of the greatness of God's majesty and nothing of Christ's triumph on the Cross. But Piper is ignoring biblical truth and deceiving his listeners. The Bible, from beginning to end, emphasises man's duty to obey God's Commandments and condemns disobedience as a great wickedness against God.

Scripture Condemns Disobedience

Adam was cast out of Eden because of his disobedience to God's first commandment. 'Hast thou eaten of the tree, whereof I commanded thee that thou shouldest not eat?... Therefore the LORD God sent him forth from the garden of Eden, to till the ground from whence he was taken. So he drove out the man...' (Genesis 3.11, 23-24).

In Deuteronomy God instructs Israel in the blessings that come from obedience, and the curses that result from disobedience. 'But it shall come to pass, if thou wilt not hearken unto the voice of the LORD thy God, to observe to do all his commandments and his statutes which I command thee this day; that all these curses shall come upon thee, and overtake thee' (Deuteronomy 28.15). They disobeyed and Scripture records the consequences.

King Saul disobeyed God many times. 'And Samuel said, Hath the LORD as great delight in burnt offerings and sacrifices, as in obeying the voice of the LORD? Behold, to obey is better than sacrifice, and to hearken than the fat of rams' (1 Samuel 15.22). The consequence of Saul's disobedience was that God rejected him as king of Israel.

The prophet Jeremiah brings the word of the Lord to Israel: 'Because they have forsaken my law which I set before them, and have not obeyed my voice, neither walked therein... I will scatter them also among the heathen, whom neither they nor their fathers have known: and I will send a sword after them, till I have consumed them' (Jeremiah 9.13,16). Ultimately Judah's disobedience led to their exile in Babylon.

Ephesians 5.6: 'Let no man deceive you with vain words: for because of these things cometh the wrath of God upon the children of disobedience.' Paul makes no reference to a lack of 'preferring', or of 'losing a taste' for God.

The peril of Piper's teaching is that he is seeking to persuade Christians that it is not important to obey God's moral law. The result is a church of disobedient, antinomian adherents who 'prefer' the pleasures of God and who reject His Commandments as unimportant.

Conclusion

This study has presented clear and compelling evidence, using his own words, that John Piper is an antinomian. His antinomianism, while at times blatant, is usually subtle, even disguised and hard to detect. In chapter 1, when responding to a question about antinomianism, his response was to plead ignorance and ask for a definition: 'Oh, for definitions, please, definitions!' He then muddied the waters with a host of absurd definitions. As a trained theologian he knows the accepted meaning of antinomianism, yet he chose to avoid the question. This evasiveness is unworthy of a Christian leader.

We have seen evidence from three videos (freely available on the Internet) of his downgrading the moral law and making it subservient to 'preferring God above all things' as the great key that unlocks the glories of the Christian life. Piper's whole ministry is built on his radical new doctrine of so-called Christian Hedonism, first presented in his 1986 book, *Desiring God*, which teaches that seeking pleasure and happiness in God is the single most important duty for all believers. 'Delight yourself in the Lord' from Psalm 37.4 is his motto text, taken totally out of context, yet held up as a literal commandment of God. It logically follows that pursuing pleasure in God comes before keeping the moral law. Obeying God's moral law is seen as secondary to seeking pleasure in God.

Christian Hedonism is predicated on antinomianism. Piper maintains that the happy Christian life flows from 'delighting' in God, and 'preferring God above all things'. He does not teach that we need to use the moral law as a rule of life to grow in godliness. Rather, he teaches that taking pleasure in God leads to a happy, satisfying Christian life.

In summary, in seeking to answer the question posed in chapter 1 (Is John Piper an antinomian?), our study has revealed the following. Piper publicly asserted that Christians are not under the Ten Commandments, thus revealing his support for antinomianism. He used an allusion to Romans 6.14 ('we're not under the law') – often regarded as the proof text for antinomianism – to support this position. He insisted that commandment-keeping is at a 'lower level' for the Christian. In three public-domain videos he made numerous antinomian statements. He said, 'law-breaking is *not* your main problem'. He said, 'The inner essence of our depravity is our *preferring* – very important word – our *preferring* the glory of created things over the glory of God and Christ.' He claimed, 'The ultimate essence of evil is the loss of taste for God as our all-satisfying life and joy, and the *preference* for other things above God himself.' He argued that the Fall was not the breaking of God's first commandment to man, but of man losing his taste for God, and desiring something other than God. He said, 'I'm not mainly interested in whether you break laws, I'm mainly interested in whether you love God or not, or love His stuff.' He said with great emphasis, 'I just want to *keep smiting*, that's what Christian Hedonism is. It's the *smite on morality.*' He wants Christians to be gripped by what he refers to as 'joyful inner impulses' from 'inside', that is, the heart. Although he qualifies this with the phrase 'of the gospel', he gives no warning of the dangers inherent in following the human heart. He openly declared that obeying God's moral law is not important. He openly said that rebellion against God's Commandments is not an issue of first importance.

All these statements are the product of an antinomian mindset which disregards the moral law as a guide to holy living. Rather, Piper wants believers to rely on subjective emotional responses from 'inside', to desire God above all things, and to take all their pleasure in God. This way of thinking, in his mind, generates true sanctification.

Piper's Christian Hedonism is deceptively appealing to the unwary, as all true believers regard the Lord as their 'chief joy'. It contains obvious truths, subtly mixed with error. Similarly, the fatal appeal of Piper's antinomianism is that it is so plausible—it seems so spiritual. Who wants to be a mere law-keeper when we can be in love with God? The profound error in his system is that it places pleasure in God above obedience to God's holy law. It replaces God's own objective rules for holiness with man's subjective inner impulses. While we are saved by grace, through faith alone, in Christ alone, we live by obedience to our Saviour, who said: 'If ye love me, keep my commandments' (John 14.15). Piper's Christian Hedonism demands he be an antinomian—the two stand or fall together.

In view of the evidence presented, we can declare with confidence that John Piper is a deeply committed antinomian. His dogma of Christian Hedonism is built on the heresy of antinomianism, which is why he can never admit to the charge. And what is most shocking is that he is teaching his antinomianism to literally hundreds of thousands of young people. It is surely time for the evangelical Church to react to Piper's antinomianism by warning Christians, especially the young, to reject his ministry and avoid his books and videos. It is surely time for Church leaders to end the eulogies of Piper and to have the courage to call him out as a false teacher.

Endnotes

1. Desiring God website, Piper address, 'The Ultimate Essence of Evil: The Majesty of God, the Triumph of Christ, and the Glory of Human Life', 3 January 2017, https://www.desiringgod.org/messages/the-ultimate-essence-of-evil

Other Books by ES Williams

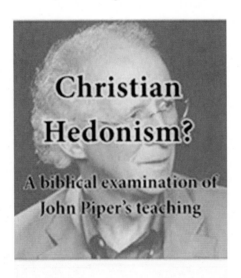

Christian
Hedonism?

A biblical examination of
John Piper's teaching

ES Williams

Many people sense that there is something profoundly wrong with combining the Christian Faith with the philosophy of hedonism, but few people are able to explain why Christian Hedonism is a false doctrine. This short book sets out to evaluate John Piper's teaching in the light of Scripture. We see how he amends the Westminster Shorter Catechism to say that 'the chief end of man is to glorify God *by* enjoying Him forever'. We see how he creates a new commandment, 'Delight yourself in the Lord', from Psalm 37.4, and then tells Christians that the vocation of their lives is to seek maximum pleasure in God. We observe how he extols the worldly worship of a Passion Conference. We learn of his new definition of love as 'holy, divine Eros'. We note how he cleverly 'digs up' Scripture to find a 'happy God'. We see how Scripture is twisted to make the claim that the apostle Paul and the Lord Jesus Himself were Christian hedonists. This book provides clear evidence that antinomianism is the underlying error upon which Christian Hedonism is built.

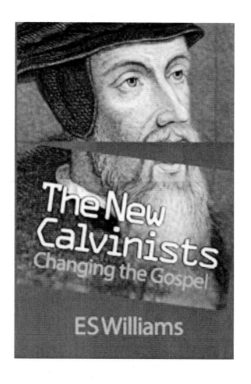

Enmity between the church and the world dates from the Fall of man, so God says in Genesis 3.15. Satan's major strategy is the overthrow of the church by the world, through infiltration and contamination. But seldom has this battle reached the proportions of this present hour, when worldliness threatens every believer and church. And so subtle is the enemy that fatal compromise now comes with an appearance of sound doctrine - in an apparent resurgence of the very best of Reformation and Puritan teaching. This book reveals the new 'gospel' of the so-called 'new Calvinism'. It is a gospel that changes the terms of salvation, and that loves the world and embraces its culture. Here are the objectives of the new Calvinists, taken from their own words.

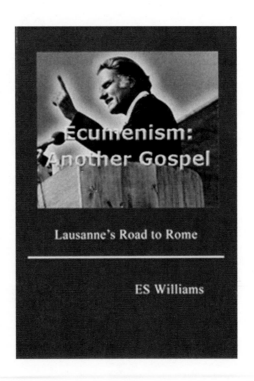

Ecumenism:
Another Gospel

Lausanne's Road to Rome

ES Williams

The Lausanne Movement is a worldwide network committed to the cause of 'world evangelization', founded by two of the biggest names in Christianity, American evangelist Billy Graham and British theologian John Stott. The Movement, which was established in 1974 in Lausanne, Switzerland, has introduced a new way of doing evangelism that combines social activism with the message of salvation — called 'evangelization'. Over the years the ecumenical ambitions of the Movement have become increasingly obvious, as many within it seek to work closely with the Church of Rome